Dynamic Duos

BY DAVID MOORE

Dynamic Duos

BY DAVID MOORE

SCHOLASTIC INC.

New York   Toronto   London   Auckland   Sydney

ISBN 0-590-12079-4

© 1998 by NBA Properties, Inc.
All rights reserved. Published by Scholastic Inc.

12 11 10 9 8 7 6 5 4 3 2 1   8 9/9 0 1 2 3/0

Printed in the U.S.A.
First Scholastic printing, February 1998
Book design: Michael Malone

TABLE OF CONTENTS

It Takes Two.......................................6

Malone & Stockton...................................10

Webber & Howard...................................18

Mourning & Hardaway...............................26

Garnett & Marbury.................................34

Jordan & Pippen...................................42

Mutombo & Laettner................................50

O'Neal & Jones....................................58

Olajuwon & Drexler................................66

Robinson & Duncan.................................74

IT TAKES TWO

Chicago's Michael Jordan stands center court after winning another championship. A few moments later, it is announced that Jordan has added one more NBA Finals Most Valuable Player trophy— and the car that goes with it—to his collection.

Jordan doesn't hesitate to welcome teammate Scottie Pippen into this elite circle. The two stand side-by-side, celebrating the Bulls' fifth title in the last seven years.

"We're a tandem," Jordan says. "It's hard to split us up. It's hard to take the MVP by myself. I'll take the trophy. He can have the car."

Jordan is spectacular. He dominates the NBA and captures the imagination like no one before him.

But basketball is a team sport. It doesn't matter how high a player can fly or how many points he can score. No player—not even one as talented as Jordan—can win a title alone.

Jordan's career has received a major assist from Pippen. His subtle brilliance is the perfect complement to Jordan. It's difficult to imagine one without the other. Together, Jordan and Pippen have assured that the Bulls will be remembered as one of the best teams of all time.

It's a terrific tandem. But this sort of one-two punch isn't an exception in the NBA. It's the rule. Teams that feature two quality players working in concert are ahead of the game—and the competition.

It's no coincidence that Chicago's opponent in the Finals last year was Utah, a team carried by the diverse skills of Karl Malone and John Stockton. The way these two respond to each other on and off the court is special.

Jordan and Pippen. Malone and Stockton. These pairings are destined to find their way into the Hall of Fame. But there are other tandems in the league, young and old, anxious to carve their own niche in the sport's history.

Miami's fortunes are on the rise now that point guard Tim Hardaway and center Alonzo Mourning have found each other. Minnesota emerged from its long playoff slumber thanks to the youthful enthu-

siasm and talent of Kevin Garnett and Stephon Marbury. Chris Webber and Juwan Howard, an act that first played to fab reviews in college at Michigan, now serve as the cornerstones of the Washington Wizards.

An odd couple (Dikembe Mutombo and Christian Laettner) have joined forces in Atlanta, while an older couple (Hakeem Olajuwon and Clyde Drexler) keep Houston going strong. Eddie Jones has watched his career with the Los Angeles Lakers take off since the arrival of Shaquille O'Neal. Two of the tallest structures in South Texas find themselves together on the same front line as the San Antonio Spurs reap the benefits of David Robinson and Tim Duncan.

These are some of the more successful and entertaining duos in the league today. Trades will create more. Time will nurture others. But one thing is certain: One star is not enough.

It takes two.

MALONE & STOCKTON

SPECIAL DELIVERY

Karl Malone wasn't looking for a lasting relationship. He simply wanted a place to sit.

That was easier said than done. There were more than 300 athletes jammed into the cafeteria that day in 1984. All had hopes of representing the United States in the Olympics. Malone, a self-described "good ol' country boy" from Louisiana, was trying to make the basketball team.

Malone finally found an empty chair. Across from him was a point guard from a small school named Gonzaga. Malone remembers thinking the guy looked kind of wimpy. But he figured the guy had to be pretty good. Karl introduced himself.

The player was John Stockton.

"Out of all those tables, we sat down at the same one and started talking," Malone says. "It's kind of amazing, really. Maybe it was fate or something."

It's hard to argue with fate. It's even harder to argue with what Malone and Stockton have accomplished.

The Utah Jazz selected Stockton in the first round of the NBA draft that same year. They took Malone one year later. Since then, the two have forged one of the most productive alliances in league history.

The two have combined to appear in a total of 19 All-Star Games. Each has won two gold medals. Stockton is the NBA's all-time leader in assists and steals. Malone was the league's Most Valuable Player last season.

Neither shows any sign of slowing down. The careers of both players are intertwined. Malone and Stockton will one day find themselves in the Hall of Fame.

Side by side.

"I've never really thought about not playing with

Karl," Stockton says. "I don't think I'd want to. Our individual talents seem to complement each other, so why kill the goose that lays the golden egg just because you want more attention for yourself?"

Frank Layden, the president of the Jazz, refuses to take credit for putting Malone and Stockton together. He calls it "an act of God."

He's right. Malone feeds off Stockton's ability to get him the ball on the break and inside. Stockton thrives because of Malone's ability to catch a pass in traffic and finish a play.

"Anything I can do in life that can be with Karl Malone, I'm thrilled by it...The more things we can share, the better for me."
—John Stockton

The entry pass to a post player is a skill often taken for granted. What if Stockton didn't have a knack for making that pass? Malone, who has a nice touch, might be forced to float outside and shoot more jumpers. In that scenario, his scoring average and field goal percentage likely would fall.

And what if Malone weren't able to establish inside position and catch the pass? For one thing, he wouldn't draw as many double-team defenses. That means Stockton, who is one of the better three-point shooters in the league, might not have had as much incentive to improve his outside shot. That ability to spread the defense has made Stockton even more effective when driving to the basket.

"I guess it has been a natural progression that has allowed both of them to adapt to each other because of their strengths," Utah coach Jerry Sloan says. "A good player adjusts to who he's playing with. That's just a part of basketball." And a part of what makes these two special.

Sloan believes Malone and Stockton would have developed into All-Stars even if they weren't on the same team. That's certainly true. But there's no question each player has benefited from the other's presence.

"There's a country saying, 'You can't have the chicken without the egg,'" Malone says. "I don't know. Is John the chicken or the egg? That's why you can't gauge what we mean to each other."

Their careers have been remarkable. But each player got off to humbling starts.

The Jazz promised free colas and hot dogs to lure a few hundred fans to the arena for the draft in 1984. Layden went to Sam Battistone, the owner of the franchise at the time, and asked him to announce the pick.

"Just as he got 'Stockton' out of his mouth, there were boos," remembers Scott Layden, Frank's son and the club's director of basketball operations. "Soda cups were flying at him along with hot dogs and wrappers.

"Sam turned around, went back to my dad and said, 'Thanks a lot. Now I know why you wanted me to announce the pick.'

"The fans, I think they thought we had drafted [announcer] Dick Stockton."

Stockton—the player—showed promise, but spent his first three-and-a-half seasons as a backup to Rickey Green. He became a starter during the 1987-88 season. That marked the first of nine consecutive seasons he would lead the league in assists.

Opposing players and coaches talk about the feel Stockton has for the game. Frank Layden talks about John's sixth sense. He maintains that Stockton does more than see the floor. He knows who is running the wings and anticipates when and where to make the pass.

And he's tough. Stockton learned the game in his family driveway in Spokane, Washington, in fierce one-on-one games with his older brother. The rivalry was so intense that neighbors referred to the two as Cain and Abel.

Stockton, at 6-1, 175 pounds, is not an imposing figure. Every summer, when Malone returns to Summerfield, Louisiana, friends come up to him and say they "could take Stockton." He just laughs. Malone and every other player in the NBA knows that Stockton, who turns 36 in March, is one of the most physical guards around.

After Stockton's three-pointer eliminated Houston in the Western Conference Finals, Rockets forward Charles Barkley went as far as to call Stockton one of the five best players he has ever competed against.

"He does three things well," Barkley said. "He's mentally tough, he can beat you scoring and he can beat you with assists. That really makes him a great player. He does all the little things.

"Karl Malone is the best player on Utah, but John Stockton is the most valuable."

CAREER HIGHLIGHTS

Karl Malone
- NBA MVP: 1997
- Fifth player in league history to score at least 25,000 points and pull down 10,000 rebounds in his career, joining Wilt Chamberlain, Kareem Abdul-Jabbar, Moses Malone and Elvin Hayes
- Selected to the All-NBA First Team for nine consecutive seasons

John Stockton
- All-time NBA career leader in assists and steals
- All-Star Game MVP: 1993 (John shared the award with teammate Karl Malone.)
- Two-time Olympic gold medalist: 1992, 1996

Malone, meanwhile, was the 13th player taken in the 1985 draft. The Louisiana Tech star stepped into the starting lineup right away and finished third in the balloting for Rookie of the Year.

Few players possess Malone's combination of size and strength. His physique looks as if it is chiseled out of marble. His offseason training routine—in which he runs five to 10 miles a day on country roads in Arkansas and lifts weights in a tin shed without air-conditioning—is legendary.

Malone, who turns 35 in July, is arguably the best power forward ever to step on the court. He has been named to the All-NBA First Team for nine consecutive years. Chicago's Michael Jordan is the only active player who has poured in more NBA points.

"He's probably improved as much as anyone could from where they started out," Sloan said.

"For five years now, I have been anwering questions about Stockton and Malone. 'Have they lost a step? How much longer are they going to be able to play?'

"I don't think anybody knows that. I don't think anybody knows how they take care of themselves, either. They've always come to camp in better condition than anyone on the team."

Their personalities are as different as their games. Malone is flamboyant. Outgoing. He has appeared in a movie and shown up on *Entertainment Tonight.* His face is plastered on virtually every billboard within 50 miles

"There's a country saying, 'You can't have the chicken without the egg.' I don't know. Is John the chicken or the egg? That's why you can't gauge what we mean to each other." —Karl Malone

of Salt Lake City, endorsing all kinds of products. Malone loves being in the public eye and is impulsive.

A few years ago, when a woman mistook him for a porter at the Salt Lake Airport, he carried her bags to the car. Malone didn't reveal his identity until the woman tried to tip him.

Stockton is much more reserved. He has few endorsements and says he wouldn't have those if his wife, Nada, didn't want him to maintain at least some sort of profile. Stockton is never rude to reporters, but he is clearly not comfortable talking about himself. He resents the media's demands on his time and doesn't understand their fascination with what he might have to say.

Which is not to say he is dull. Stockton often imitates the mannerisms and quirks of teammates and coaches. He also likes to play practical jokes.

In the early 1990s, before a game with Charlotte, Stockton walked up to Malone and told him he saw one of the Hornets go on TV and say the Jazz power forward was overrated.

Malone went out and scored 52 points. After the game, when reporters pressed Stockton to reveal the identity of the Charlotte player, he admitted he had made it up.

There are other differences. Malone loves to hunt. Stockton has never shot an animal. Stockton has no desire to drive an 18-wheel truck around the country the way Malone has in past summers.

Still, these two have become close friends. They sit next to each other on the team bus and plane. Stockton is the godfather of Kadee Lynn, Karl Malone's oldest daughter. Malone has spent time with Stockton and his family in Spokane.

"Stock, to me, is the neatest guy," Malone says. "I really don't know of a better person to know and talk to than him.

"In this day and age, with professional athletes and grown men, it's one of those things people think is corny, for men to be close like we are."

Stockton doesn't find it to be corny at all.

"Anything I can do in life that can be with Karl Malone, I'm thrilled by it," Stockton says. "We have become great friends, and I think our friendship has grown.

"The more things we can share, the better for me."

WEBBER & HOWARD

A FAB REUNION

Chris Webber doesn't say a word. All it takes is a glance. He spins past his defender, plants his left foot and leaps toward the basket.

A lob pass from teammate Juwan Howard is waiting. These two communicate more with one look than some people do during a five-minute conversation. Webber traps the ball in his right hand and rattles the rim as he slams it home.

This has become Webber and Howard's signature play. It was developed in college during their days with the Fab Five at Michigan. It is being perfected on an almost nightly basis as the two continue their careers. Webber and Howard, the cornerstones of one of the most celebrated college teams of the 1990s, have now joined forces with the Washington Wizards.

"There's no problem with me finding him on the court," Howard said. "We surprise some people. They wonder, 'How can two forwards play so well together, always find a way to see him on the transition?'

"Because we know each other and we've been playing so well together ever since the days at Michigan. I've never played so well with anyone like that before. Also, because we have two guys who are very unselfish and believe in winning."

It has been a long time since the Washington franchise has done much winning. The Bullets—the club changed its name to the Wizards recently—won the NBA title in 1978. Some lean years followed.

Washington had gone eight consecutive years without making the playoffs. It had lost 50 or more games six times in that span.

The drought ended last season. The Wizards won their final four games of the regular season to finish 44-38 and meet Chicago in the first round of the playoffs. Webber and Howard played major roles. Their reunion has helped resurrect interest in the NBA in the nation's capital.

Webber is the flashier of the two. His skills border on physical genius.

Howard is steadier, more reliable. He is the one who sacrifices the most, the one who alters his game, to make this association work.

"People ask me about being in Chris' shadow," Howard said. "I've never felt that way. To me, being on the same team as Chris Webber has been the best thing that ever happened to me."

The tale of how these two wound up together—twice —is interesting.

Howard was born to a 17-year old who lived in the projects on the south side of Chicago. She couldn't afford a crib. After being brought home from the hospital, Howard spent the first week of his life sleeping in a dresser drawer with a pillow for a matress.

Jannie Mae, Howard's grandmother, and the daughter of Mississippi sharecroppers, wound up raising him. Howard was 6-8 by the time he reached high school. His team at Chicago Vocational High practiced in an unheated gym and didn't have a locker room. The players suited up for home games in a history classroom.

The facilities weren't the best. Still, Howard soon was regarded as the best big man in Chicago. He would sign a letter of intent to play for Michigan.

What started out to be the best day of his young life ended in tragedy. After signing the letter and holding a press conference at his school, Howard rushed home to share the rest of the day with his grandmother. That is when he learned Jannie Mae had suffered a massive heart attack. She had slumped over the kitchen table and died a few hours earlier.

He later had Jannie Mae's name tattooed over his heart.

"People ask me about being in Chris' shadow. I've never felt that way. To me, being on the same team as Chris Webber has been the best thing that ever happened to me." —Juwan Howard

Howard was the first member of the Fab Five—the nickname of the five freshmen who led the Michigan Wolverines to the NCAA championship game in their first year—to commit. He quickly got on the phone and recruited Jimmy King. Ray Jackson and Jalen Rose followed.

The last to buy into the program was Webber.

"Chris and I played against each other in the summer leagues," Howard said. "We didn't like each other much, because we were both big men. It was a natural rivalry.

"But when I went to Michigan and I saw that we were recruiting Chris, I called him several times. I told him that if he came, we could win a national championship right away."

Webber came from a hard-working, middle-class family in Detroit. His father was an auto worker; his mother an elementary school teacher. The day he scored 64 points and had 15 dunks during an eighth grade game, it was clear he was something special.

Jalen Rose and Webber became friends in the seventh grade. But Webber attended Detroit Country School rather than Southwestern High. Rose taunted his friend for being soft because he attended a rich, suburban school. That didn't keep Webber from leading the school to three state championships.

Webber was the star of the Fab Five. Their talent, baggy shorts, shaved heads and black shoes and socks took college basketball by storm. And there was that attitude.

"We were the guys in the black hats, but we liked it," Webber said. "We were criticized a lot. Some of the things that were said about us on TV would make my mother cry. But it never bothered us, because all five of us felt like we were in it together."

The Fab Five advanced to the Final Four in each of their first two seasons at the school. They played in the title game each time.

They lost each time. Michigan trailed North Carolina by two points with 11 seconds left in their sophomore year when Webber called a timeout the Wolverines didn't have. Michigan was slapped with a technical foul, the Tar Heels sunk two free throws and celebrated a title seconds later.

"When you look at the big picture, you get bigheaded," Webber said. "And when you get bigheaded, God humbles you. The Timeout."

Webber, the last of the Fab Five to sign, was the first to go. A few weeks after the Timeout, he declared for the 1993 NBA Draft. Orlando took him with the first pick— the first sophomore to be selected No. 1 since Magic Johnson 14 years earlier—and immediately traded him to Golden State for Anfernee Hardaway and three future first-round picks.

Webber was named the league's Rookie of the Year. He became the first player in league history to total more than 1,000 points, 500 rebounds, 250 assists, 150 blocked shots and 75 steals in his first season. But he and Don Nelson, then the coach of the Warriors, didn't get along. It soon became clear he wouldn't play a second season with Golden State.

Howard, meanwhile, was taken by Washington with the fifth pick of the 1994 draft. Contract negotiations were tense—at one point Howard broke down and cried —and the forward held out to start the season.

Back on the West Coast, Webber had given the Warriors a list of six teams for which he would play. Washington, because of Howard, was one of them.

CAREER HIGHLIGHTS

Chris Webber
- First NBA rookie with more than 1,000 points, 500 rebounds, 250 assists, 150 blocked shots and 75 steals
- Schick NBA Rookie of the Year: 1994
- First-time NBA All-Star: 1997

Juwan Howard
- One of only five players in Michigan history to score at least 1,500 points and grab 750 rebounds for his career
- Two-time NBA All-Star: 1996, 1997
- NBA All-Rookie Second Team: 1995

On November 17, 1994, Washington traded for Webber and signed Howard. Owner Abe Pollin called it "one of the biggest days in the thirty-year history of the franchise." The Wizards sold nearly 1,200 season tickets in the next 24 hours. It normally took the club an entire summer to sell that total.

A new, exciting era had begun. Not only did Webber

"When you look at the big picture, you get bigheaded. And when you get bigheaded, God humbles you. The Timeout."
— Chris Webber

and Howard give Washington hope on the court, but they made an impact in the community as well. Webber's Timeout Foundation—his mother came up with the name, thinking it was funny—helps kids in the Washington, D.C., and Detroit area. Howard formed a similar foundation for kids in D.C. and Chicago and frequently visits children in hospitals.

Howard also became the first NBA player to leave school early and still receive his degree on time. He completed the 32 credits he needed in communications during his rookie year by carrying books on road trips and faxing his assignments to professors.

"I want everybody to know that a college degree still has some value," Howard said. "You always hear about a lot of players leaving school for the big money in the NBA. But they rarely go back to get their degree.

"Hopefully, some of the NBA players will look at what I've done. I mean, they don't have to finish their education in one year. You can take your time. It's hard work, but you can get it done."

It hasn't all gone smoothly for Webber and Howard in Washington. The team was 21-61 in their first season. The Wizards won 39 games the next season and fell just short of a playoff berth.

Webber wasn't a part of the playoff push. A dislocated shoulder that required season-ending surgery limited him to just 15 of the team's 82 games. His maternal grandfather died and a close friend became critically ill.

"The only way I stayed strong was Juwan did well," Webber said.

Howard averaged 22.1 points, 8.1 rebounds and became an All-Star during the 1995-96 season. But Webber's absence was noticed.

"I was like a lost puppy without him," Howard said.

The two were back together last season to lead the Wizards into the playoffs. Losing to the Bulls in the first round did nothing to dampen their enthusiasm for what lies ahead.

We're going to do some things here," Webber promised. "I'm looking forward to it."

MOURNING & HARDAWAY

THE HEAT IS ON

The blueprint is on file in the front office of every NBA club. The best way to build a team is to put a strong center and point guard in place. Once this foundation is laid, the chances of constructing a team that can contend for a championship increase.

The problem is there aren't enough quality centers and point guards to go around. Most teams are forced to make do with one or the other and build from there.

The Miami Heat refused to settle for Plan B. One of the first moves Pat Riley made after taking over as the Heat president and head coach was to trade for Alonzo Mourning. He followed that three months later with a deal that brought Tim Hardaway into the fold.

Mourning is a young star on the rise. Hardaway is a veteran who has overcome a major knee injury to regain his All-Star form. These two give the Heat much more than talent. They provide an attitude, an edge, that Riley demands.

"You've got to have two or three guys to take the load off of everybody else," Hardaway said. "It's always easier to build around a center and a point guard.

"Me and Zo, we have that confidence to go out there and do whatever we can to get our team the W, just like Michael and Scottie. Our teammates look for us to do that."

In their first full season together, Mourning and Hardaway led Miami to 61 wins and the Atlantic Division title. The Heat advanced to the Eastern Conference Finals for the first time in their history before losing to Chicago.

The two combined to average 40.1 points a game. Hardaway led the team in scoring, assists and steals.

Mourning led in rebounds and blocked shots. They also began to form a bond.

Mourning said the relationship between him and Hardaway grew stronger because they are the focal points of the team's success. Mourning believes the two are beginning to develop the sort of friendship that Utah's Karl Malone and John Stockton share.

"We think of ourselves as a tandem," Hardaway said. "But I really don't look at it and try to compare myself and him to other tandems. I don't look at that stuff. I just want us to be on the same page every game of the season."

The same page isn't always enough. Riley expects his players to be on the same sentence. What he has seen from Mourning and Hardaway so far pleases him.

"They have a good feeling for each other and it will get better," Riley said. "That takes time. It takes hundreds and hundreds and hundreds of possessions. Then you start to read each other better. You know when to make the post entry passes, things of that nature. The lob is a read you make after you get to know each other.

"You get forty points a game between the two and there is some upside, because I think there is a lot of upside to Zo's game."

Life wasn't easy for Mourning growing up in Virginia. His parents were on the verge of a divorce. There was a lot of tension.

At the age of 10, the courts gave Mourning the option to leave his parents and enter a foster home. He took it and moved in with a woman named Fannie Threet, who had taken in more than 200 children in her time. Threet encouraged Alonzo to build a good relationship with his parents, even though he no longer lived with them. He did. Mourning talks about how his parents remained supportive and helped teach him right from wrong.

Basketball didn't come easy, either. He was awkward,

"I think because things didn't come easy for me at a young age, hard work and determination were qualities I developed." —Alonzo Mourning

even clumsy, for his age. That was made even worse by the fact his clothes didn't fit, and the other kids laughed at him.

Mourning decided the best way to make the kids stop laughing was to work harder than them. It's a trait he retains today. Mourning has been known to call the Heat strength-and-conditioning coach on a Saturday or Sunday evening at 10 o'clock to join him for a two-hour workout.

"I think because things didn't come easy for me at a young age, hard work and determination were qualities I developed," Mourning said.

He's also developed one of the sport's meanest glares. The look is designed to intimidate opponents or discourage people from approaching him. Mourning, like his good friend New York's Patrick Ewing, is intense. He wants to push aside those things in his life he believes distract from his ability to focus on basketball.

"He doesn't like small talk or wasting somebody's time," Riley said. "But Zo really is very gregarious. He's an affable, fun guy. He just wants to be that way in a protected environment.

"Kareem [Abdul-Jabbar] was the same way. As soon as he walks out of the locker room, Zo does pull that shade down."

Hardaway is more outgoing. But like Mourning, he is driven to prove people wrong.

The player nicknamed "Tim Bug" was thought to be too small to make a big impact in college. The University of Texas at El Paso was the only major college that wanted to take a chance on this point guard who barely stood

CAREER HIGHLIGHTS

Alonzo Mourning
- First player to be named Big East Player of the Year, Defensive Player of the Year and Big East Tournament MVP in the same season
- Second overall pick in the 1992 NBA Draft
- Four-time NBA All-Star

Tim Hardaway
- NBA All-Rookie First Team: 1990
- Fifth player in league history to average at least 20 points and 10 assists in consecutive seasons, joining Oscar Robertson, Magic Johnson, Isiah Thomas and Kevin Johnson
- Named to All-NBA First Team: 1997

6 feet. He went on to be the school's all-time leading scorer and was named the Western Athletic Conference Player of the Year as a senior.

Hardaway burst onto the NBA scene at Golden State and was admired for his deadly crossover dribble. But he missed the entire 1993-94 season with a torn anterior cruciate ligament in his left knee. Again, there were doubts. Would Hardaway be the same explosive player he was before the injury?

It took some time—and a trade from Golden State to Miami—but Hardaway is back. The Heat point guard isn't as explosive as he was earlier in his career, but he is more effective. He flourished in the Warriors fast break, open-court style and now with the halfcourt sets preferred by Riley.

"I can run a team," Hardaway said with pride. "If you want me to run up and down the court, I can do that. If you want me to slow it down, I can do that."

He does whatever Riley asks.

"He's such a competitor," Riley said. "He's the closest thing I've been around to Magic Johnson. He's a six-foot Magic Johnson, that's what he is."

Miami lost very little ground in the standings last season after Mourning tore a tendon in his right arch. The reason was Hardaway refused to let them slide. Riley went so far as to campaign for Hardaway for the Most Valuable Player Award.

"He's such a competitor. He's the closest thing I've been around to Magic Johnson."
— Heat coach Pat Riley on Tim Hardaway

"The thing is Tim Hardaway has never been linked in the context of Michael Jordan and Karl Malone and those players," Riley said. "This year, his name should be linked with MVP. Tim Hardaway is as legitimate as everybody else. Will he get it? Probably not."

Hardaway didn't win the award. It went to Malone. But he did join Jordan in the backcourt on the All-NBA First Team.

Even more important, he began to build a relationship with Mourning.

"They take the responsibility for leadership and they have grown close together," Riley said. "From that standpoint, it's been a real good pairing."

A pairing that should carry the Heat into the next century.

"We feel that we have a special nucleus," Hardaway said. "I'm part of something that's going to be great this year, next year and in the years to come.'"

GARNETT & MARBURY

TIME TO HOWL

Geography and age kept the two apart. When one grows up in New York and the other in South Carolina, it's hard to get together and hang, especially when neither guy is old enough to drive.

Yet these weren't your typical high school students. Stephon Marbury knew there was something special about Kevin Garnett the moment he saw this 6-11 prodigy do a crossover move on an ESPN highlight. Garnett, meanwhile, had heard of this "Mayberry kid" from Brooklyn. The scouting report: He couldn't shoot, but he sure was fast.

The two had never met. But it seems each kid saw a little bit of himself in the other. When Marbury was around 15 years old, he got Garnett's telephone number and gave him a call.

They never got off the phone. Marbury and Garnett talked about everything. Ball. Girls. School. Ball. Girls. The two became close friends.

The phone bill in the Garnett household reached $80 one month. Kevin had to give his mother, Shirley, half of his check from his first week of work at Burger King just to cover the cost.

These days, the phone bills aren't nearly as expensive. Garnett and Marbury see each other every day at practice with the Minnesota Timberwolves. The two sometimes chill at the Mall of America or play pool and video games at Garnett's home.

It appears Garnett and Marbury were destined to be together. The Timberwolves are just thankful fate—along with the draft and a key trade—led both to Minnesota.

"One day they will dominate at their positions," said Kevin McHale, the 'Wolves vice president of basketball operations.

That day may not be far away.

Garnett was the first player in 20 years to jump directly from high school to the NBA. He appeared in the All-Star Game in his second season.

Marbury left Georgia Tech after his freshman season to join Garnett. He made a strong push for Rookie of the Year, an award eventually won by Philadelphia's Allen Iverson.

Together, Garnett and Marbury helped thaw a Minnesota franchise that was in a deep freeze. The Timberwolves made the playoffs for the first time in their existence last season and are viewed as a team on the rise.

This is clearly one of the most exciting young tandems in the league. But if you want to compare Garnett and Marbury to some other successful duos in operation, forget it.

"We're Garnett and Starbury," Garnett said, referring to his nickname for his friend. "We want people to some-day compare other people to us. That's where we're try-ing to get."

And they're trying to get there as friends.

"Friendship is important because you can tell each other the truth right away," McHale said. "Friends cut to the chase, and in a forty-eight-minute basketball game, you'd better cut to the chase.

"I like that aspect of Kevin and Stephon. These guys play unselfish ball. They think of themselves as basketball players, not quasi entertainers."

Minnesota coach Flip Saunders calls Garnett "a physical freak." It's a compliment.

Few players Garnett's size are as graceful as this 21-year-old athlete. He can slash to the basket and dunk over almost any defender. He has a nice turnaround jumper in the low post. His perimeter game has improved.

Scoring. Rebounding. Blocked shots. Garnett can take

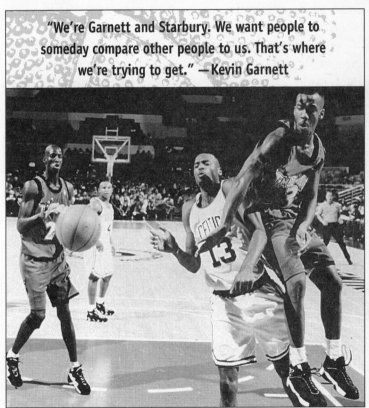

"We're Garnett and Starbury. We want people to someday compare other people to us. That's where we're trying to get." — Kevin Garnett

control of a game in any of these areas. The only small forward in the league who has as big of a defensive impact on a game is Chicago's Scottie Pippen.

In the words of Saunders, Garnett is a player who "can carry a team."

"He has such a tremendous will to succeed," McHale said. "He knows there are a lot of people out there who would like to see him fail because a high school kid shouldn't come into the league and succeed.

"So he's really driven, very self-motivated and very tough on himself, like all great players are."

Teammates and opponents marvel at how good Garnett has become at such a tender age. Minnesota guard Terry Porter said it doesn't take a genius to see that the fifth player taken in the 1995 draft is something special.

Garnett takes pride in the fact he's made it at an early age when some people thought he couldn't. He's the voice of a generation, saying young players "like to run and gun and alley-oop and holler and jump up and down." He talked with Chicago's Michael Jordan during the All-Star Game, telling His Airness he was going to "be caught up in a KG special" if he didn't watch out.

"I know I can be one of the best players out there," Garnett said. "I hope that doesn't sound cocky. Come on, man, watching me play—if I wanted to score, don't you think I could?"

The game is fun. That is why Garnett plays. It's not for the money or the crowd.

It's also his medicine. When Garnett is depressed or things aren't going his way, he always has basketball. Jordan has said the same thing.

"When I didn't have a friend, when I was lonely, I always knew I could grab that orange pill and go hoop," Garnett said. "I could go and dunk on somebody. If things weren't going right, I could make a basket and feel better."

Marbury comes from a family that lives and breathes basketball. His three older brothers all played college ball and had dreams of making it in the NBA.

CAREER HIGHLIGHTS

Kevin Garnett
- Named High School Player of the Year by *USA Today*: 1995
- First player in more than 20 years to be drafted by an NBA team out of high school
- First-time NBA All-Star: 1997

Stephon Marbury
- Named National High School Player of the Year by *Parade* magazine: 1995
- Fifth player in Atlantic Coast Conference history to be selected All-Conference First Team as a freshman
- NBA All-Rookie First Team: 1997

None did. Eric played at Georgia and is now working in construction. Don Jr. played at two junior colleges and Texas A&M. He earned a degree from Weber State and is also in construction. Norman went to a junior college and has played professionally in Indonesia.

Stephon is the one who fulfilled the family dream. He was named National High School Player of the Year by *Parade* magazine. He was the ACC Rookie of the Year and became the first freshman to lead Georgia Tech in scoring since NBA All-Star Mark Price.

Garnett prodded Saunders and McHale to watch Marbury every time the Yellow Jackets had a game.

Saunders and McHale teased Garnett every time Iverson had a good game. But the more the Timberwolves scouted Marbury, the more they liked him. When he announced he was leaving Georgia Tech after one season, the club had a strong interest.

"Kevin kept telling me we had to get his boy, and I'd told him that we'd love to," McHale said. "But the problem was we were batting fifth and weren't sure his boy was going to be around long enough for us to get a swing at him."

"If I can throw a sweet pass, that's better than anything. It's like getting a jumper and a dunk. You advance in three categories. You've made yourself feel good, made that player feel good, and the team scored." —Stephon Marbury

Iverson went to Philadelphia with the first pick of the 1996 draft. Toronto took Marcus Camby with the second pick while Vancouver selected Shareef Abdur-Rahim third.

Milwaukee had the fourth pick. Minnesota struck a deal to send the fifth pick (Ray Allen) and a future first-rounder to the Bucks for Marbury. The Timberwolves had a draft pick who was genuinely happy he wound up in Minnesota.

Marbury is explosive off the dribble. He doesn't

pound or dominate the ball and looks to get those around him involved.

"I know I make every player around me better," Marbury said. "I come to the game and show people what they want to see. I'm not too flashy, but I can be flashy if I want to be. I can be flashy when it's necessary. I play hard defense all the time. I have a lot of pride and I love scoring."

"If I can throw a sweet pass, that's better than anything. It's like getting a jumper and a dunk. You advance in three categories. You've made yourself feel good, made that player feel good, and the team scored."

There are times Marbury misses New York. But he calls Minnesota the perfect place to play basketball because there are no distractions and he can watch a lot of tape.

In that way, Marbury and Garnett are alike. Neither are caught up in their image as much as they are trying to improve.

"If we can keep them together," Saunders said, "eventually we should play for the championship."

The trick may be keeping them together. While Garnett has already signed a long-term contract, Marbury is eligible to become a free agent at the end of the 1998-99 season.

Minnesota knows it isn't a slam dunk that Marbury will stay. Several teams would love to make a strong push to sign him. Minnesota hopes his relationship with Garnett—along with a fat contract—will keep the two together for a long time.

"They're hungry," McHale said. "They want to be great players. And they're not jaded by anything."

HAND IN HAND

He was so weak before the game he had trouble putting on his uniform. He lacked the energy to talk to his teammates at halftime. There were times in the second half when he almost fainted.

Somehow, he still found the strength to score 38 points and lead his team to victory.

Chicago's Michael Jordan has made the impossible seem routine throughout his career. But what Jordan did in the Finals last year was remarkable even by his standards.

It was his 19-foot jumper at the buzzer—over the outstretched arms of Utah's Bryon Russell—that lifted the Bulls to a victory in the first game of the series. It marked the 23rd time His Airness had won a game for Chicago with a basket or free throw on the team's final possession.

Eleven days later, with the series tied 2-2, Coach Phil Jackson was afraid a stomach virus would keep Jordan from playing. His 38 points won the game and changed the complexion of the series.

"Michael's legacy continues to grow," Bulls teammate Scottie Pippen said. "As long as he plays the game, he's going to amaze us no matter what, because he has the ability to take control of the game, to make the big shot, to make the big play.

"I just see no end of the rainbow for a guy of Michael's caliber. Physically, he probably is as healthy and physically ready as a twenty-five-year-old player. We never feel like he's going to meet his top potential. He's the guy who continues to rise. No matter what's out there, he's been able to overcome it.

"No matter how you look at it, he's the greatest to ever play this game and he proves it, night in and night out."

Once again, Jordan took center court. When the series was over, the Bulls had won their fifth title in seven years. Jordan, who lost the Most Valuable Player Award to Utah's Karl Malone during the regular season, walked away with the MVP trophy in the Finals for the fifth time.

The legend keeps getting bigger. But this was also the Finals where Pippen emerged from Jordan's shadow to take his place next to the sport's best player.

It began in Game 1. Jordan's shot proved to be the game-winner. But the Bulls wouldn't have been in a position for Jordan to make a difference if it weren't for Pippen. He finished with 27 points and was easily Chicago's most consistent performer. He had nine rebounds, two assists, three steals, four blocked shots and played more minutes (43) than his healthier teammates.

Pippen did all this despite an injured left foot that prevented him from working out with the Bulls in the two days leading up to the series.

"He gave us a courageous effort," Jordan said. "In the first half, I know he was thinking about the injury and the pain. In the second half he came out and became aggressive. He picked up the intensity a little bit. He carried us."

If Pippen hadn't played, Chicago's sputtering offense would have lost the game. His three-pointer with 1:11 remaining—after Jordan was double-teamed on the baseline—gave the Bulls an 81-79 lead and was the second biggest shot of the evening.

"It's that part of the season where you want to do everything you can to stay above water and not sink," said Pippen, who refused to be dragged down by the soft tissue damage to the bottom of his foot. "I wanted to do whatever I could. I was in pain, but I was able to overcome."

That has not always been the case. Pippen's migraine headache during a decisive playoff loss to the Detroit Pistons in the late 1980s sparked derisive comments

"He's my closest friend on the team. There isn't anything I wouldn't do for him." —Michael Jordan

about his will to win. His refusal to enter a playoff game with 1.8 seconds remaining in 1994 because the final play wasn't called for him soiled his reputation.

Pippen's performance in the Finals against the Jazz helped push those memories aside. It also served as a reminder of what he does best.

It was Pippen's defense on Earvin "Magic" Johnson of the Los Angeles Lakers that helped turn the tide in Chicago's favor in its first title of the 1990s. It was his defense on Utah's John Stockton that helped lift the Bulls to their fifth.

CAREER HIGHLIGHTS

Michael Jordan
- Four-time NBA MVP: 1988, 1991, 1992, 1996
- Won five NBA titles and five NBA Finals MVP Awards: 1991, 1992, 1993, 1996, 1997
- Nine-time winner of NBA scoring title

Scottie Pippen
- All-Star Game MVP: 1994
- Two-time Olympic gold medalist: 1992, 1996
- All-NBA First Team three times

Stockton averaged 17 points, 12 assists and three turnovers in Utah's two victories. In its four losses, those averages dropped to 13.9 points, 7.6 assists and 4.3 turnovers. Stockton had 13 points and five assists in the final game.

But it wasn't just what Pippen did to Stockton. The Bulls small forward finished with 23 points and nine rebounds in Game 6. His three-pointer with just more than 10 minutes remaining gave Chicago its first lead since early in the first quarter. His spectacular block of

Shandon Anderson's layup with 7:12 left sent the fans at the United Center into a frenzy.

"A lot of people watch scorers, and Michael is one of the best scorers in this game," Jackson said. "But Scottie's defense was a one-man wrecking crew.

"People who see the game as a whole see what he does on the basketball court. He rebounds, delivers the basketball, organizes the offense and puts in a few baskets of his own to boot. Scottie really delivered for us.

"They're such a tag team. It's a joy to watch them play."

Jordan and Pippen have won five titles and nearly 75 percent of their games in their first nine years together. No other tandem in the history of the sport has a better winning percentage.

Still, these two were not always close. Jordan often referred to the Bulls as his supporting cast early in his career, a phrase that bothered Pippen and others. There was some jealousy over all the attention Jordan received.

Jordan, meanwhile, often felt he had to do too much on his own. He felt the pressure was always on him to come up with a big fourth quarter or the play at the end of a tight game because no one else would step up.

Their relationship changed in the year-and-a-half Jordan walked away to play baseball. Suddenly, Pippen was the man. When Jordan returned with 17 games left in the 1994-95 season, Pippen had a better understanding and appreciation of the load Jordan was asked to carry.

"It's a different feel of the game when you don't have such a great, dominant player," Pippen said. "If you don't have that one guy in there who draws all the attention, the double-teams, it allows a team to load up on you."

Jordan treats Pippen with more respect than he did in the past. He treats him as an equal. When Pippen's name comes up in trade discussions, Jordan has made it clear to management that he wouldn't want to return to a team without his small forward.

> "I think we both sense if one of us is going well, we continue to let that person go at it until it's time for the other one to step up. We do it naturally. We know each other so well, it's just instinct." —Scottie Pippen

MALONE & STOCKTON

WEBBER & HOWARD

MOURNING & HARDAWAY

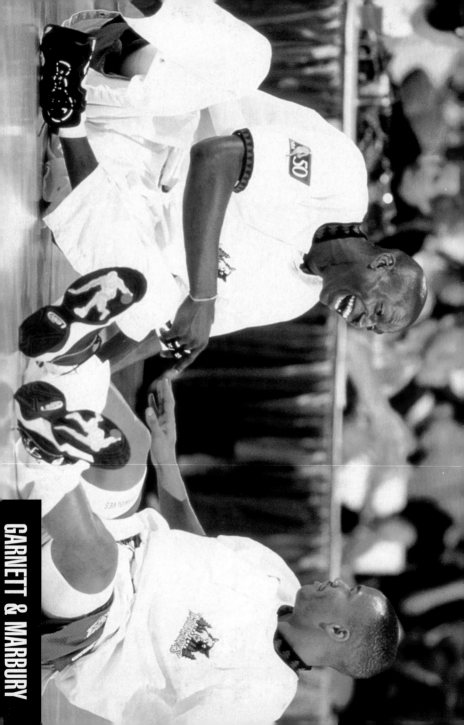

GARNETT & MARBURY

JORDAN & PIPPEN

LAETTNER & MUTOMBO

O'NEAL & JONES

OLAJUWON & DREXLER

The two have finally found peace with their relationship and their place in this dynasty.

"I know when he's shooting the ball well and has a great rhythm, I want the ball to be in his hands," Pippen said. "I know he's a very difficult player to defend. He's going to cause a lot of problems for the defense, and sooner or later he's going to open up opportunities for others on the court.

"I think we both sense if one of us is going well, we continue to let that person go at it until it's time for the other one to step up. We do it naturally. We know each other so well, it's just instinct."

Jordan kept his MVP trophy from the Finals, but gave Pippen the car that goes with the award. It wasn't the first time he has made such a gesture. Jordan gave Pippen his Ferrari as a Christmas present six months earlier.

"He's my closest friend on the team," Jordan said. "There isn't anything I wouldn't do for him, and I'm pretty sure it's vice versa. We've gone through adversity and still survived and come out with a positive view on life."

Pippen gave Jordan an earring that same Christmas. It was a diamond-encrusted replica of the NBA championship trophy.

"He looks after me like a big brother," Pippen said. "Whatever he has, he feels he can share it with me. I think I have a special relationship with him."

MUTOMBO & LAETTNER

BIRDS OF A FEATHER

Dikembe Mutombo's deep, rich voice rumbles through the Atlanta locker room like thunder.

Mutombo had just been informed that the coaches included him on the All-Star roster for the fourth time. His excitement increases when he discovers Hawks teammate Christian Laettner will be making his first appearance.

"I am so happy," Mutombo roars. "I'm going to the game with my new, white brother."

Mutombo and Laettner are vastly different personalities. Mutombo is an entertaining soul with a heart as big as his size-20 shoe. He will talk about anything from basketball to politics and is quick to laugh.

Laettner is not nearly as outgoing. His intensity and lack of humor rubs some people the wrong way. The forward developed a reputation as being surly and hard to get along with during his days at Duke and Minnesota.

The Hawks have not seen that side of Laettner. Mutombo's gregarious nature and Atlanta's rise in the Eastern Conference standings have helped people view Laettner in a different light.

"There were a lot of bad things said about Christian," Mutombo said. "People used to say he didn't have a personality, he didn't have this, he didn't have that. But maybe they did something to give him a headache in Minnesota. I would say to anyone, Christian is a great guy."

Laettner returns the compliment. "I didn't know how good his personality would be," he said of Mutombo. "When he steps on the court, you know he's going to block shots, you know he's going to get some dunks and hook shots.

"But I like Dikembe best because of what he brings to the locker room and on the bus, in the hotel. He's very charismatic. When he walks on the bus, when he walks in the room, he jacks everybody up. That's what I like about Deke the most."

Dikembe Mutombo Mpolondo Mukamba Jean Jacque Wamutombo grew up in Kinshasa, Zaire. He came to the United States as an exchange student in 1987. His goal was to become a doctor.

"I did not come to play basketball," said Mutombo, who speaks English, French, Portuguese, Spanish and five African dialects. "I came to be educated."

He wound up doing both. Several people at the U.S. State Department who had seen Mutombo went to Georgetown coach John Thompson and told him of this 7-2 giant who had just enrolled at his school. Thompson met with Mutombo and invited him to join the Hoyas basketball team.

Mutombo was soon given an athletic scholarship. He changed from premed to a double-major in diplomacy and linguistics.

He excelled on and off the court. Mutombo was named the Big East Defensive Player of the Year his final season and finished his career as the school's all-time leader in field goal percentage (.644). He spent one summer on Capitol Hill as an intern for Robert Matusi, Democratic congressman from California, giving him a chance to work on his term paper, "U.S. Policy Toward the Third World." The next summer, Mutombo worked at the World Bank, translating French into English and operating computers.

"I did not come to play basketball. I came to be educated." —Dikembe Mutombo

Denver selected Mutombo with the fourth pick of the 1991 draft. He spent his first five years in the league with the Nuggets before signing with Atlanta as a free agent before the start of the 1996-97 season.

Mutombo and several other Atlanta players visited an Indian reservation with Hawks general manager Pete

53

Babcock before the start of the season. Mutombo knows more about handling a Lexus than he does a horse, but that didn't stop him from offering riding tips to the youth gathered around him in the corral. All of a sudden, Mutombo kicked the horse and the animal bolted. When the horse refused to heed Mutombo's commands to stop, he dropped the reins and jumped off.

Luckily for the Hawks, Mutombo's defensive instincts are more polished than his equestrian skills. He won his second Defensive Player of the Year Award in three years, finishing second in the league in rebounding (11.6) and blocked shots (3.3).

Mutombo's presence in the middle allowed Coach Lenny Wilkens to mold the type of aggressive, defensive team he wanted since joining the Hawks five seasons ago. His personality has energized an otherwise reserved group.

"The personality of the team has changed," Babcock said. "This is a good, solid group of guys, but they had a quiet personality as a team. We are more extroverted now, and that comes through Dikembe."

CAREER HIGHLIGHTS

Dikembe Mutombo
- NBA All-Rookie First Team: 1992
- First player in history to lead the league in blocked shots for three straight seasons: 1994, 1995, 1996
- Two-time NBA Defensive Player of the Year: 1995, 1997

Christian Laettner
- First player to start in four consecutive NCAA Final Fours
- NBA All-Rookie First Team: 1993
- First-time NBA All-Star: 1997

Laettner made a name for himself on the college level. His teams were 123-15 in his four years at Duke. He became the first player to start in four consecutive Final Fours. The Blue Devils won the title twice and Laettner became the NCAA Tournament all-time scoring leader with 407 points.

That success didn't follow him to the NBA. Minnesota used the number three pick of the 1992 draft on Laettner. The Timberwolves were one of the league's worst teams, and his arrival didn't make much of a difference. Laettner feuded with teammates and got into confrontations with assistant coaches. He played for four coaches in his first three-and-a-half years in the league and labeled two of them "rinky-dink" because they failed to exercise leadership.

This unflattering picture was much different from the one Duke coach Mike Krzyzewski had of his former star.

"I love Christian," Krzyzewski said. "He was the best player I coached in college. Grant Hill was the most talented. Bobby Hurley was the most daring. But Christian Laettner was the best. He always wanted the ball in pressure situations."

Laettner was traded to the Hawks on February 22, 1996. He was so happy to receive a fresh start that he flew to Atlanta the evening the deal was completed. It turned out to be the change his career needed.

"I heard so many bad things about him," Hawks guard Steve Smith said. "I didn't know what to expect. But I haven't seen anything like that. Maybe his problem was he couldn't get used to losing."

Maybe. Laettner also became frustrated because he

said the players didn't get along and they didn't play well together. He felt people looked toward him to be the savior of the franchise, and he couldn't do it.

"I think I fit in pretty good with the Hawks. I'm at peace with myself." —Christian Laettner

It is clear Laettner is much more relaxed in Atlanta. Mutombo talks about how Laettner has found a happiness that was missing in Minnesota.

"I think I fit in pretty good with the Hawks," Laettner said. "I'm at peace with myself."

And his position.

At 6-11, 245 pounds, Laettner has always felt he is a power forward. But he was forced to play center the majority of his time with the Timberwolves and when he first arrived in Atlanta. The acquistion of Mutombo allowed him to move to forward.

The two compliment each other perfectly. Laettner no longer has to bang against taller, more physical players in the middle. This gives him the freedom to do what he does best, which is help his team on the offensive end of the court.

Mutombo, meanwhile, benefits offensively because Laettner commands the double-team in the low post. He said he loves to play with Laettner because everything the forward does is with the goal of winning.

"This is the first time in my life I'm playing with a quality big man," Laettner said. "I'm on a great team and I'm playing great basketball. That's all I ever wanted."

O'NEAL & JONES

HIGH HOPES

Ten fingers. No rings. Shaquille O'Neal reminds his adoring public of that finger-to-championship ratio in one of his many commercials.

With the help of Eddie Jones and the rest of his Los Angeles Lakers teammates, O'Neal hopes to acquire that piece of jewelry.

The Lakers failed to advance past the second round of the playoffs last season. Utah disposed of them on the way to the NBA Finals.

It was a disappointing end to a promising season. But that defeat did nothing to dampen the club's optimistic future. There is a belief in Los Angeles that it's only a matter of time before O'Neal and the Lakers hang another championship banner from the rafters at The Great Western Forum.

Jerry West, the club's executive vice president of basketball operations, was so moved by O'Neal's decision to choose the Lakers over Orlando in free agency last season that he said it ranked ahead of the birth of his children. Agent Leonard Armato called his client "a multimedia global icon." Magic Johnson proclaimed that the Lakers with O'Neal are more talented than the Showtime version that break-danced their way to five titles in the 1980s.

More wins. More fans in The Forum. More titles. These are the expectations generated by O'Neal's move to the West Coast.

"We have acquired a superstar, one that I feel will bring us to that level we have enjoyed in the past," West said. "There is no question, this is a rebirth.

"He has a personality to go with his enormous ability.

Los Angeles is a town with personalities, and it's a town that will embrace a person like this."

The fans *have* embraced O'Neal. So have his teammates. The Lakers have put aside their egos to make room for Shaq.

"Everybody on this team sat down, and we know who 'The Man' is," Jones said. "Shaq's going to be our man to bring home the bacon for everybody."

O'Neal may bring home the bacon, but someone has to help cook it. That's where Jones comes in. The 6-6 guard has been considered one of the league's rising stars. O'Neal's arrival merely hastened that rise.

Jones is the complete package. He's the ultimate complementary player in that he can adjust his game to fit the team's needs. Jones has been able to play off of O'Neal's strengths and enhance his own reputation in the process.

"I'm a role player on this team," said Jones, who made his first All-Star appearance last season. "Shaq's our superstar, our scorer, and I have to back him up and do the things I'm able to do to make our team go."

The role the Lakers ask Jones to play changes from game to game. Some nights, Los Angeles needs him to score. Other nights, his focus is on making the pass or shutting down the opponent's top perimeter threat.

O'Neal's overpowering presence inside is a constant. Teams know what they must try to do to lessen his impact. Jones' versatility and attitude make that more difficult to accomplish.

When teams are foolish enough to defend O'Neal with one man—as Portland did in the first round of the play-

"Everybody on this team sat down, and we know who 'The Man' is. Shaq's going to be our man to bring home the bacon for everybody." —Eddie Jones

offs—Jones is content to get the ball inside. Jones took just three shots in the playoff game in which O'Neal scored 46 points. He didn't complain. Jones said as long as the Trail Blazers tried to cover O'Neal with one man, he would get him the ball.

The Trail Blazers finally altered their defensive stance

and double-teamed O'Neal. As soon as they did, Jones burned Portland for 19 points.

Jones is at his best putting the ball on the floor and slashing to the basket. But as soon as O'Neal signed, Jones knew most teams would double-team this 7-1, 300-pound force of nature. That would leave Jones alone on the outside. In order to make teams pay—and lessen the pressure on O'Neal inside—Jones had to improve his outside shot.

"I worked my butt off over the summer," Jones said. "I didn't even go on vacation. I didn't play a lot of game situations, but I shot the ball every day—three- to five-hundred shots a day."

The result was that Jones averaged a career-high 17.2 points last season. He hit 152 shots from three-point range, just 22 less than what he hit in his first two seasons combined.

O'Neal's presence also allows Jones to gamble more on defense. He finished fourth in the league in steals with an average of 2.36. It marked the third consecutive season Jones has ranked in the top 10 in the NBA in steals.

CAREER HIGHLIGHTS

Shaquille O'Neal
- First overall pick in the 1992 NBA Draft
- Schick NBA Rookie of the Year: 1993
- Olympic gold medalist: 1996

Eddie Jones
- NBA All-Rookie First Team: 1995
- First-time NBA All-Star: 1997
- Ranked among the league's top 10 in steals in each of his first three seasons

With O'Neal and Elden Campbell, the Lakers are one of the league's best teams at blocking shots. If Jones attempts a steal and fails, he often has enough time to get back into position defensively since players are reluctant to take the ball inside.

"I think he's one of the top ten defenders in the league, and that's not just on the basis of his steals, because I've seen a lot of 'steals guys' who weren't all that good defensively," Lakers coach Del Harris said. "Eddie plays solid one-on-one defense and good team defense, too."

Harris will use Jones at both backcourt positions and small forward. He's usually asked to defend the opponent's best outside scorer. His quickness and defensive tenacity creates problems. Chicago's Michael Jordan has averaged 24 points and shot just 36 percent from the field in his four games against Jones.

Jordan spoke with Jones at a party during last year's All-Star Weekend in Cleveland. He began the conversation by saying, "So, you think you've got my number, huh?"

Jones just smiled. He takes pride in what he's been able to accomplish. But he's quick to give O'Neal credit for his aggressiveness on both ends of the court.

"I think one hundred percent of it is because Shaq is down there," Jones said. "I think being able to take chances defensively has been a big key for us. If I can get some steals, it's easier getting transition baskets.

"And then with Shaq down there, I get to take a shot whenever I like. When he kicks it out, if I'm open, I take a shot or I drive to the basket and create for someone

"I think he's one of the top ten defenders in the league, and that's not just on the basis of his steals…Eddie plays solid one-on-one defense and good team defense, too." —Lakers coach Del Harris

else. Shaq is the main part of the whole game."

O'Neal is the main part. But not the only part. Campbell and point guard Nick Van Exel also have key roles in the Lakers success.

And Jones. West gets excited talking about Jones' confidence and about how much better he can become.

"I want people to see that I have a total game," Jones said. "I can be walking down the street or riding in my car and people will say, 'Hey, man, I like your game. Keep it up at both ends of the court.' That's rewarding to me."

The differences between O'Neal and Jones are striking. O'Neal is a corporation unto himself. A tattoo on his left arms reads: The World Is Mine.

It's hard to argue. O'Neal pitches everything from shoes to diet soda. He cuts rap albums, makes movies and plays for the United States in the Olympics in his spare time. He has people to handle his fan mail and his day-to-day chores and even employs a cook.

Jones, meanwhile, does his own shopping and laundry. "Shaq's our superstar," Jones said. "I'm a background type of person."

But not too far in the background. The Lakers paid O'Neal handsomely to win a championship. He will need the help of Jones and others before he can give the club a return on that investment. "I think if we all just come out and play together and play our roles, anything is possible," O'Neal said. "We have a lot of talent on this team, some big-name players, some players who can take over games on this team...

"We have a chance."

OLAJUWON & DREXLER

SECOND TIME AROUND

The two went their separate ways after college. The luck of the draw allowed Hakeem Olajuwon to stay in Houston while Clyde Drexler wound up in Portland.

That didn't keep the two from talking. Olajuwon and Drexler were unable to win a championship while they were together at the University of Houston. Their dream was to be reunited and lead a team to the NBA title.

It was the sort of thing people fantasize about but never really believe will happen. Once it all came true, there was an overwhelming feeling of accomplishment.

"This is so special for me and Clyde," Olajuwon said after the Rockets won their second consecutive championship in 1995. "We didn't do it together in college. Then to get together twelve years later in the pros was really special."

Olajuwon and Drexler have a special relationship. The two matured during their Phi Slama Jama days—the nickname for one of the most exciting college teams ever assembled—at Houston. Olajuwon was called "The Dream." Drexler was known as "The Glide" for his graceful flights to the basket.

Both went on to All-Star careers, Olajuwon with the Rockets and Drexler with the Trail Blazers. A trade in 1995 brought them together for a title run.

That run may not be over. Olajuwon and Drexler have aged like fine wine. The addition of Charles Barkley gives Houston three of the best players in league history. If the Rockets remain healthy, they could challenge Chicago's hold on the championship trophy.

Olajuwon is still the man for the Rockets. Legendary centers Wilt Chamberlain, Bill Russell and George

Mikan have praised Olajuwon for playing the game the way they did. Rockets coach Rudy Tomjanovich said some will argue that Olajuwon is the greatest center of all time, and he is one of them.

Drexler is still amazed at what his friend can do on the court.

"When he gets going, I just stand back and smile," Drexler said. "Dream is just unstoppable when he gets on one of those runs, and it's kind of funny to watch the other team try to do something.

"It's a great situation for me to be in, because I'm so close to the action. I just give him the ball and stand back and watch."

Barkley, who was acquired before the start of the 1996-97 season, has replaced Drexler as Houston's second offensive option. But that doesn't mean Drexler has been pushed out of the picture.

The Rockets didn't trade for Barkley until Tomjanovich discussed the move with Olajuwon and Drexler. He knew Drexler would have to make the biggest sacrifice. Barkley is at his best in the low post and on the wing. Those are the two spots where Drexler has been the most effective. Barkley's arrival meant fewer shots for Drexler and the need to emphasize different parts of his game.

Drexler understood. All three understood that sharing the burden would make it easier and could prolong their careers.

There are still nights when Drexler is the key player for Houston. They just don't come as often.

"It's like you've been the CEO of a company for ten years, and then you move into a different division,"

"When he gets going, I just stand back and smile. Dream is just unstoppable when he gets on one of those runs, and it's kind of funny to watch the other team try to do something." —Clyde Drexler

Drexler said. "You have the skills to do everything, but you can be a role player where it's easier to do less. That what it's like.

"If more is needed and you get the opportunity, then you have to take advantage. But if not, you stick to the game plan and let everybody do what they do well."

CAREER HIGHLIGHTS

Hakeem Olajuwon
- First overall pick in the 1984 NBA Draft (Michael Jordan was third, behind number-two pick, Sam Bowie)
- NBA MVP, Defensive Player of the Year, and NBA Finals MVP: 1994
- Led Rockets to consecutive NBA Championships: 1994, 1995

Clyde Drexler
- Olympic gold medalist: 1992
- Won NBA Championship with the Rockets: 1995
- Portland's career leader in points, rebounds and steals

What Olajuwon and Drexler do well hasn't gone unnoticed. Olajuwon has been a part of two championship teams; Drexler one. Both have won a gold medal with the Dream Team. Both were included on the list of the 50 greatest players in NBA history that was selected during the NBA's golden anniversary.

There was nothing in the high school background of either player to indicate this sort of stardom.

Drexler drew attention to himself while at Houston's Sterling High School. He was an athletic player who appeared to defy gravity. He hung in the air while defenders were on their way down. The downside was that Drexler had no jump shot. Houston and Texas Tech were the only major programs to offer him a scholarship.

Still, Drexler seemed like a sure bet compared to Olajuwon. Soccer was his game growing up in Lagos, Nigeria. He didn't take up basketball until he was 17 years old. An international coach named Chris Pond took notice and called to ask Houston coach Guy V. Lewis if he was interested. Lewis said he would take a look.

Olajuwon flew from Africa to Houston on the slim hope he would receive a scholarship. Lewis told two of his assistants to flip a coin to see who would go to the airport to pick up this kid they had never seen. Neither went because they didn't believe the kid would show up.

A few hours later, Olajuwon pulled up in the parking lot outside of Lewis' office. He had taken a cab.

Lewis knew Drexler would be special. He was the only player Lewis ever put in the starting lineup from the first day of practice. Olajuwon was different. He played sparingly as a freshman. Lewis admits he had no idea the center would develop into one of the most dominant players of his era.

Together, these two laid the foundation for a team that would make three consecutive trips to the Final Four and play in the championship game twice during the early '80s. The school recently retired their numbers. But the NBA draft ended their days as teammates.

Both had successful careers on their own. Drexler appeared in the Finals twice with Portland, but came away without a ring. Olajuwon led the Rockets to their first title during the 1993-94 season. But Houston struggled the next season, and Tomjanovich was convinced the team wouldn't defend its championship without a major trade.

On Valentine's Day, 1995, the Rockets sent Otis Thorpe and Marcelo Nicola to the Trail Blazers for Drexler and Tracy Murray.

"Hakeem and I have talked about this for many years," Drexler said. "We were laughing like little kids when I saw him in the locker room."

Drexler was home. Four months later, Houston swept Orlando in the Finals. A city—and the members of that Phi Slama Jama team—celebrated.

"There's no question they were both definitely team

"A lot of people misunderstand. A role model is not someone who's trying to be one. You don't try. You believe in some principles, fundamental principles, where you are the same person at home that you are in public." —Hakeem Olajuwon

players," Lewis said. "They were great individual players, but they didn't let that overshadow the team concept.

"Not only are they two of the finest players I've had, but they are also two of the nicest guys you will ever meet. None of the money or fame has gone to their heads."

Both are viewed as class individuals. Both are involved in the community. While others debate whether or not a professional athlete should be held up as a role model for children, these two embrace that opportunity.

"A lot of people misunderstand," Olajuwon said. "A role model is not someone who's trying to be one. You don't try. You believe in some principles, fundamental principles, where you are the same person at home that you are in public. If you act one way at home and another way when you're in public, that's when there's pressure. There's no consistency. The consistency is in being yourself.

"We're talking about the future of our children. This is very important because this is the future of the country. If you are in a position where you can inspire others, then promote what is good. That's how you can help, and what a beautiful position to be in, where you can influence people in a positive manner.

"How can you reject that position?"

ROBINSON & DUNCAN

TWIN TOWERS

There was no drama. From the moment the machine spit out a Ping-Pong ball with San Antonio's logo, Tim Duncan knew he would be selected by the Spurs with the first pick of the draft.

Still, when commissioner David Stern actually called his name nearly six weeks later, the Wake Forest senior felt a rush.

"It's been a long time coming," Duncan said that June evening. "I got a lot more excited than I thought I was going to be."

Opponents don't share that excitement. The prospect of facing a front line that includes Duncan and a healthy David Robinson should provide headaches for years to come.

This isn't the first time two tall, talented centers will join forces in the same frontcourt. Houston featured the Twin Towers—Hakeem Olajuwon and Ralph Sampson—in the 1980s. New York experimented with Patrick Ewing and Bill Cartwright for two seasons in the late '80s.

Spurs coach Gregg Popovich is in charge of devising a scheme to maximize the talents of Duncan and Robinson. He has looked at tapes of those old Rockets and Knicks teams to get some ideas.

But don't expect San Antonio to run the same plays. Popovich stressed that these Twin Towers are more versatile than any duo that went before them.

"I think these guys are unique," Popovich said. "Basically, they are players who are adept inside and out and can run like deer.

"It's our job to use them to our best advantage."

Robinson joined the Spurs for the 1989-90 season. That is when an awkward, twelve-year-old named Tim Duncan took up basketball on his island home of St. Croix.

Duncan and Robinson talked shortly after the Spurs won the lottery. Robinson expressed his excitement. He also told the rookie he should be thankful that he gets to go to a good team where he doesn't have to be the focal point. Duncan agreed.

"I think I was really blessed to have an opportunity to go in there and win a lot of games our first year," Duncan said. "That's really different from most No. 1 picks that have to go in and rebuild a team.

"I think it'll really help me a lot. It'll give me a chance to grow with not as much pressure on me. At the same time, I can help the team in my own way."

After Robinson was drafted, the Spurs had to wait for two years while he completed his Naval obligations. This gave the club the opportunity to tailor a team around the Admiral's skills by the time he climbed aboard.

San Antonio went 56-26 in Robinson's rookie season, an improvement of 35 wins over the previous season. That remains the biggest one-year jump in league history.

There are expectations that Duncan will have a similar impact. The Spurs weren't a bad team last season, merely an injured one. Robinson and small forward Sean Elliott missed the majority of the season. Their return—and Duncan's arrival—should make a big difference.

"I think I can do a job of relieving some stress off him," Duncan said of Robinson. "It's good turning around and having somebody by your side who can really help you out defensively, on the glass. To have that

"I think these guys are unique. Basically, they are players who are adept inside and out and can run like deer. It's
our job to use them to our best advantage."
—Coach Gregg Popovich

strain on one person is a real big deal."

Popovich was determined to ease the strain on Robinson even before the Spurs won the lottery. Robinson won the league's Most Valuable Player award during the 1994-95 season when former coach John Lucas pulled the center away from the basket. Robinson would still set up in the low post, but he was just as likely to get the ball on the wing or near the free throw line.

The Spurs planned on using Robinson that way again this season. Popovich wanted him to pick up the majority of his minutes at power forward instead of center.

Duncan's presence makes that easier to pull off. Wake Forest coach Dave Odom estimates Duncan spent 80 percent of his time in the low post. He appears to be more comfortable than Robinson with his back to the basket.

Popovich stressed it's not important who spends most of his time on the block and who goes outside. The important thing is that Duncan and Robinson develop a chemistry.

CAREER HIGHLIGHTS

David Robinson
- NBA MVP: 1995
- Led the league in scoring (1994), rebounding (1991), blocked shots (1992)
- Three-time U.S. Olympian: 1988, 1992, 1996

Tim Duncan
- Became the tenth player in NCAA Division I history to score 2,000 points and grab 1,500 rebounds
- Atlantic Coast Conference Player of the Year: 1996, 1997
- First overall pick in the 1997 NBA Draft

This is what has the rest of the league worried.

"We have games that can intertwine real well," Duncan said. "We won't have defined positions. We'll just play off each other's strengths."

> "I think I can do a job of relieving some stress off him. It's good turning around and having somebody by your side who can really help you out defensively, on the glass. To have that strain on one person is a real big deal." —Tim Duncan

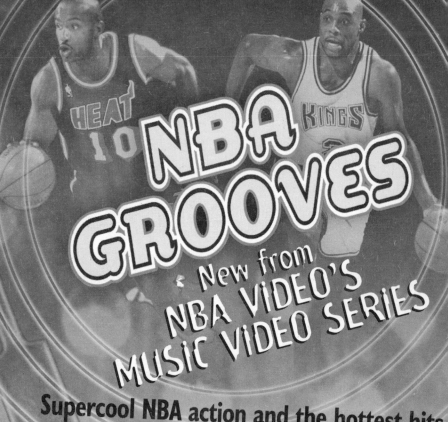